PARTS

PARTS

Shelley Rotner

HOUGHTON MIFFLIN BOSTON

Petals on top,
leaves down below

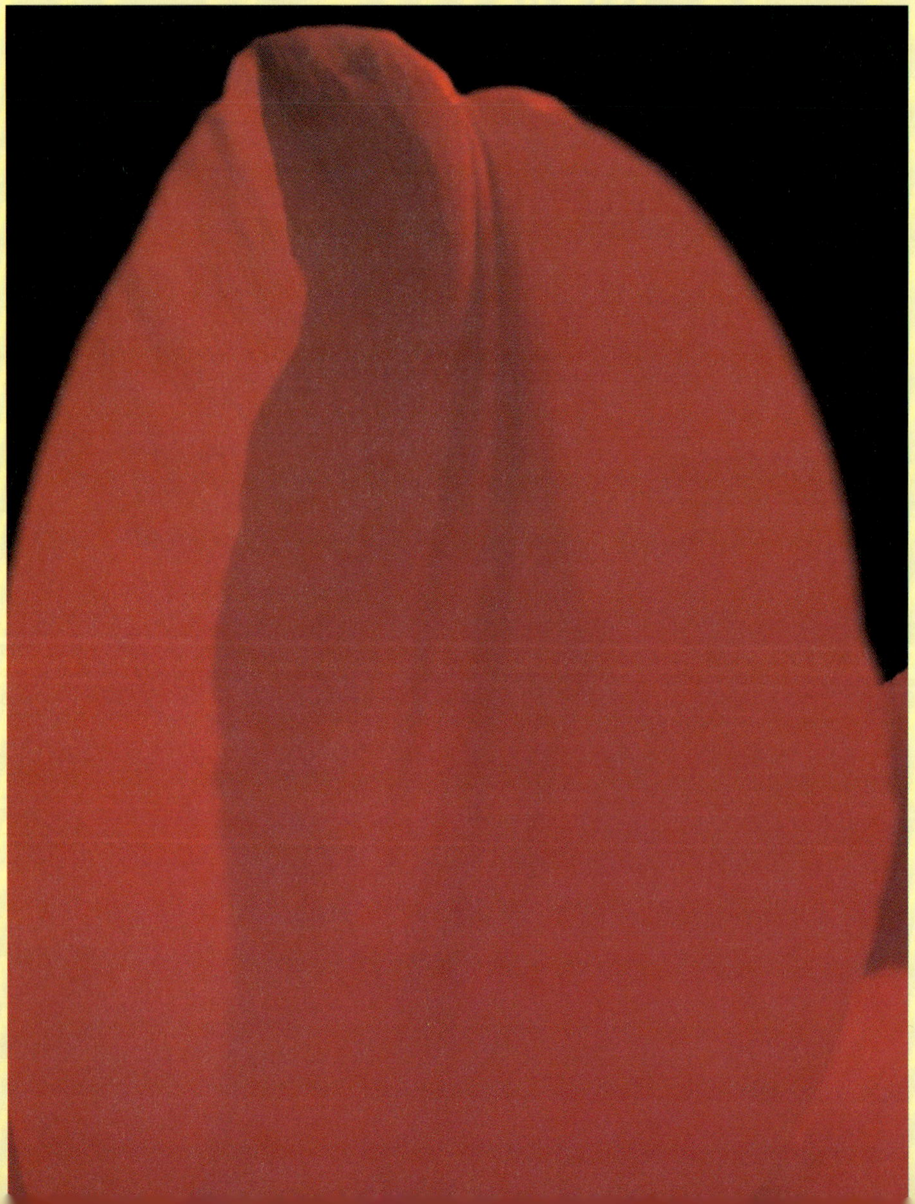

Up out of the ground
they grow

On tall green
stems stand bright
red towers

Come
and smell
the pretty
FLOWERS.

What's bright yellow, with seats in rows

Up and down the streets it goes

NORTHAMPTON

Red lights flash
when it stops for us

Climb on board the big
SCHOOL BUS.

Smooth and round
with a striped green skin

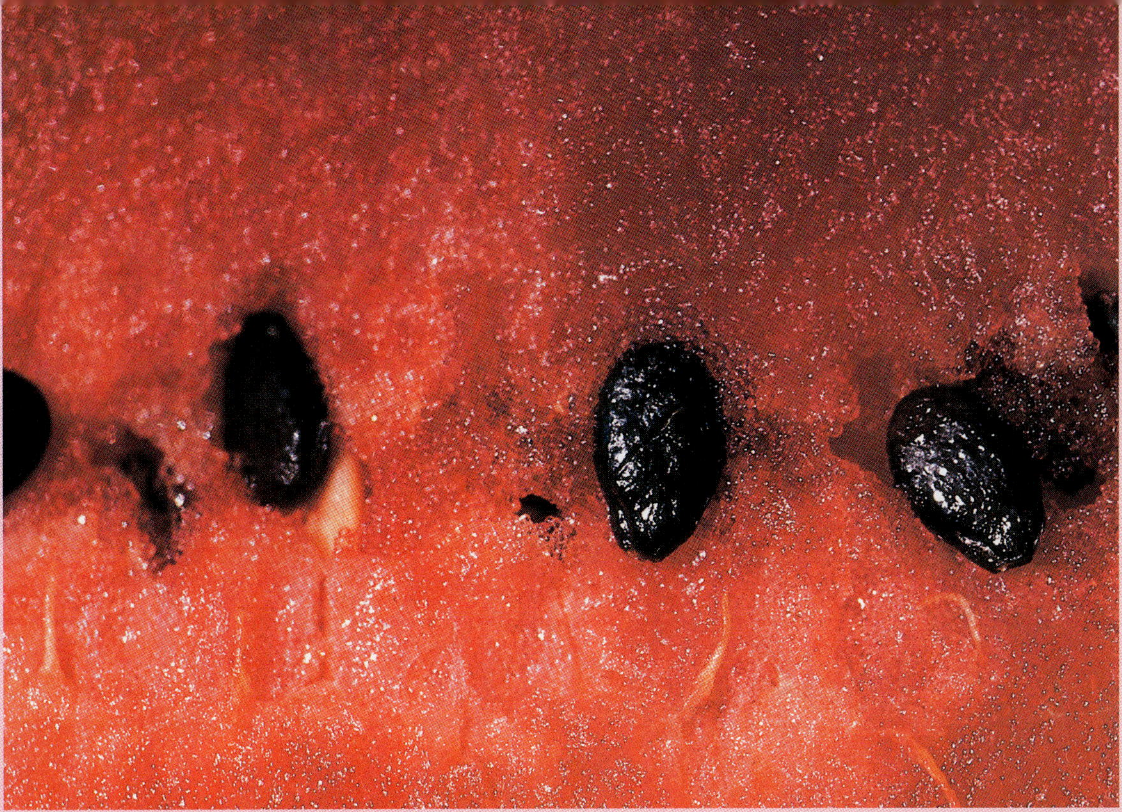

Red fruit,
black seeds hidden within

Garden ripe and
ready to eat

Taste the
WATERMELON,
juicy and sweet.

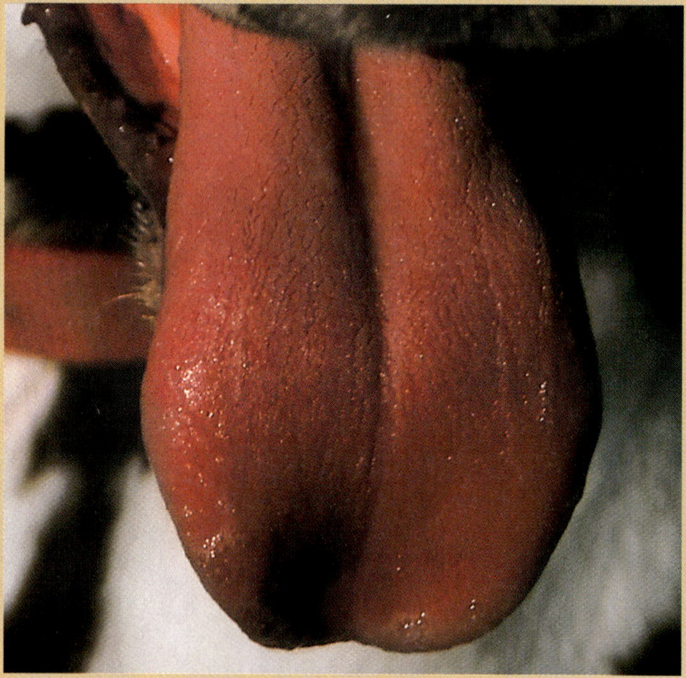

A tongue to lick, a tail to wag

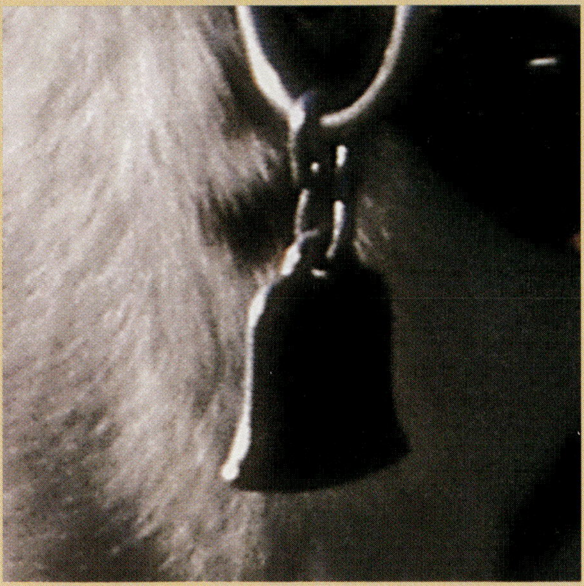

Around his neck he wears a tag

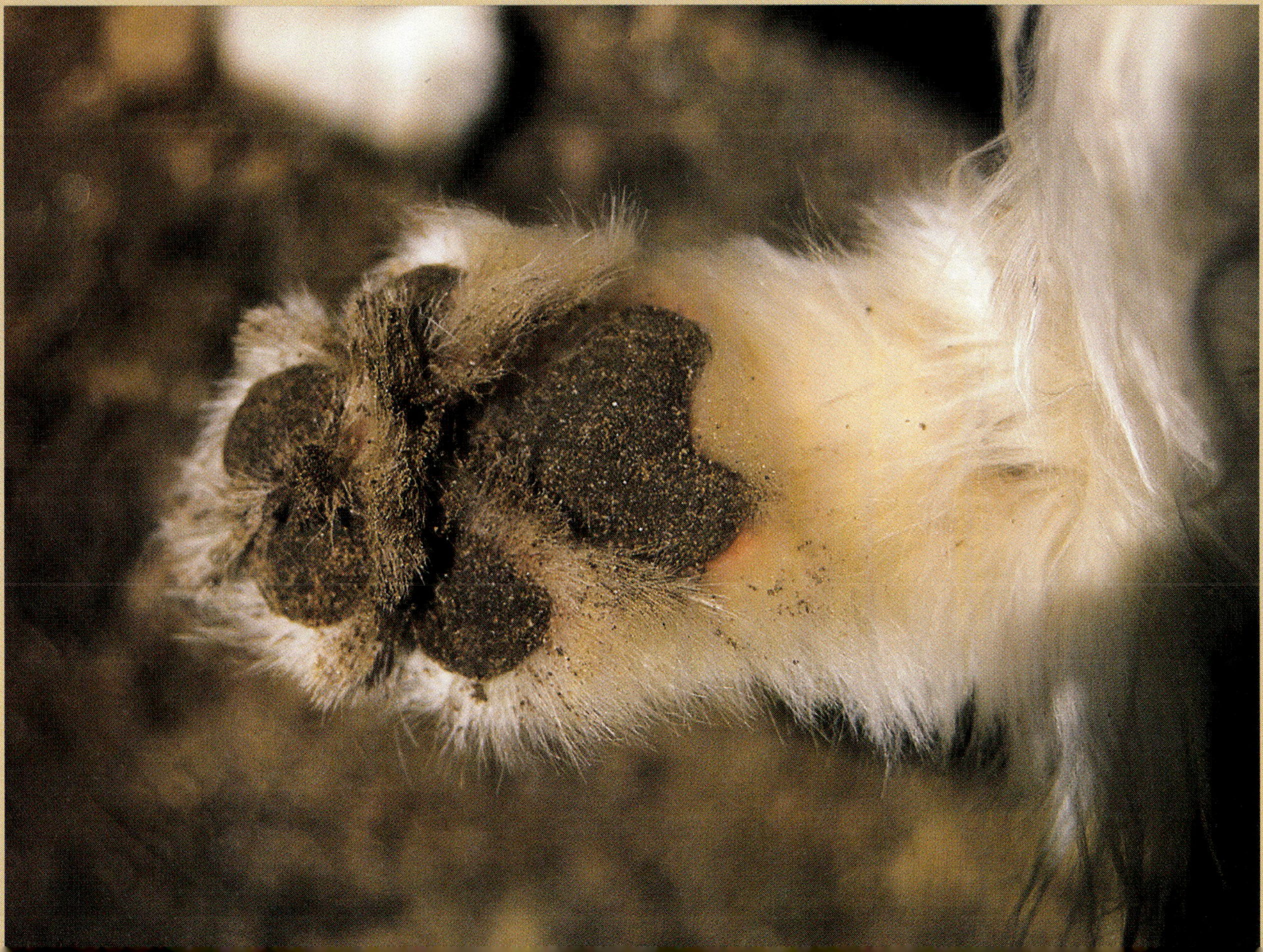

His fur is soft,
his nose is wet

A loyal
DOG
is one great pet.

Pedal hard, switch the gears

Going fast, have no fears

Ride around without a care

Your BICYCLE takes you anywhere.

Climb up the steps, one, two, three, four

Stand on the porch, knock on the door

155

I always return after I roam

To the place where I live —
my house,
my HOME.

A head
on top

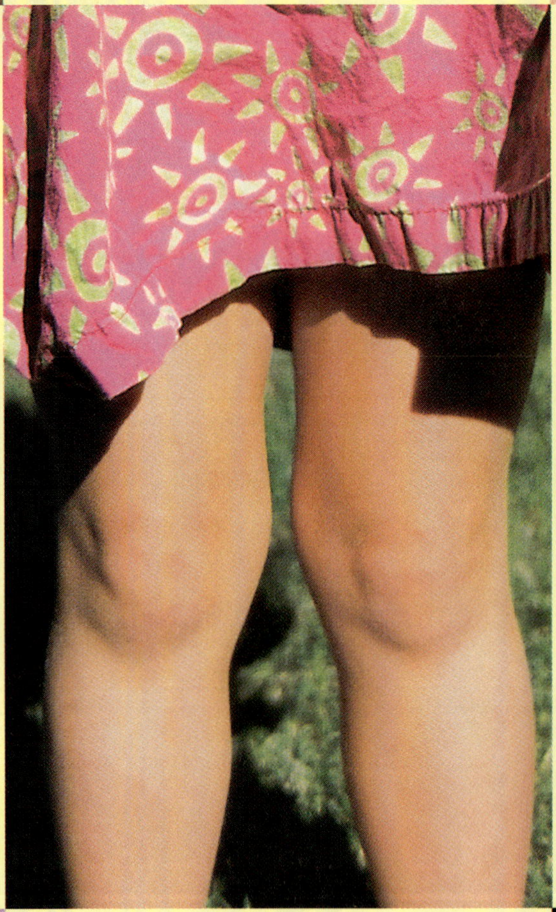

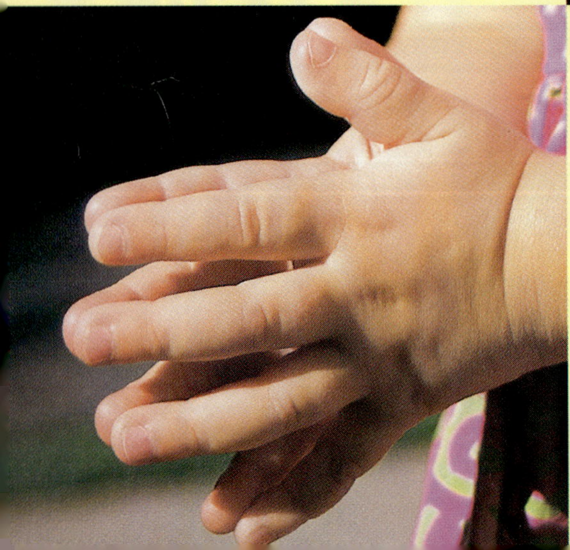

and legs
below

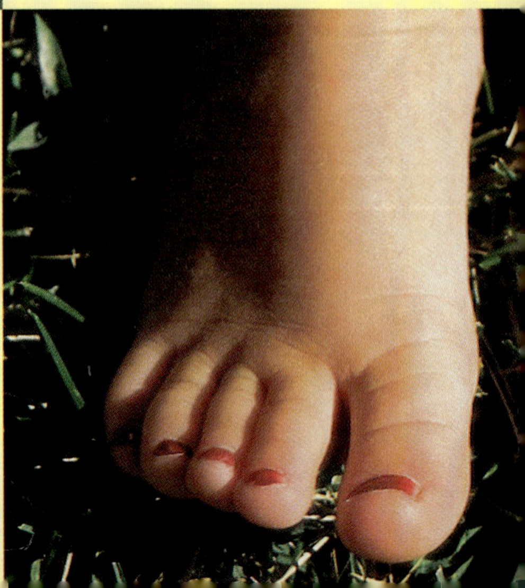

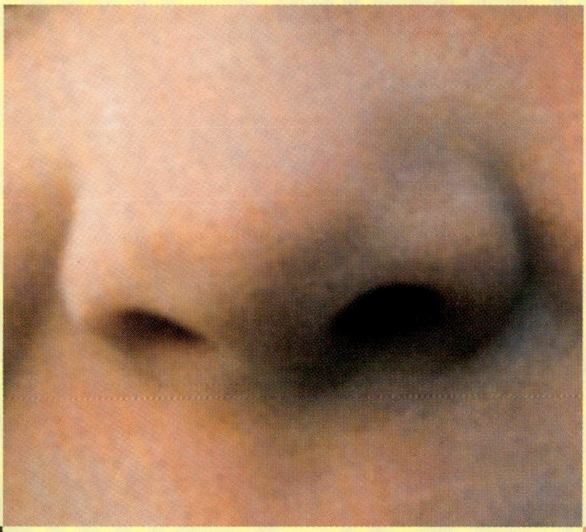

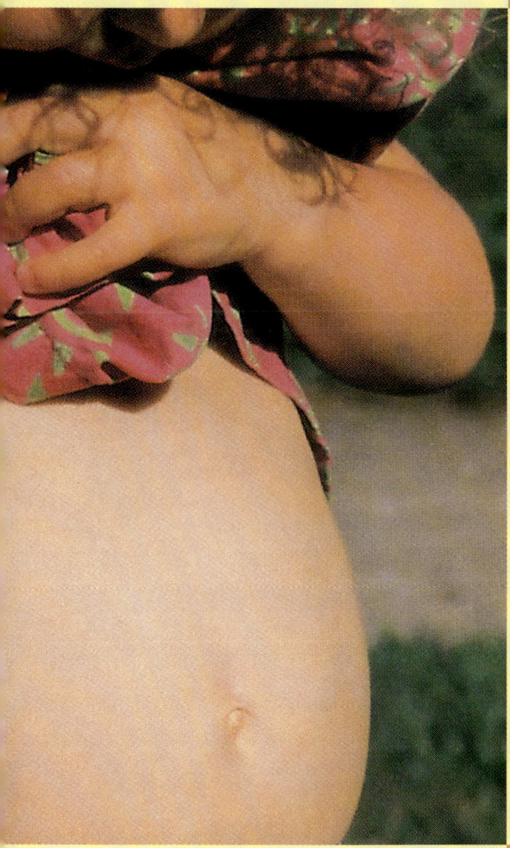

All my
parts will
grow and
grow

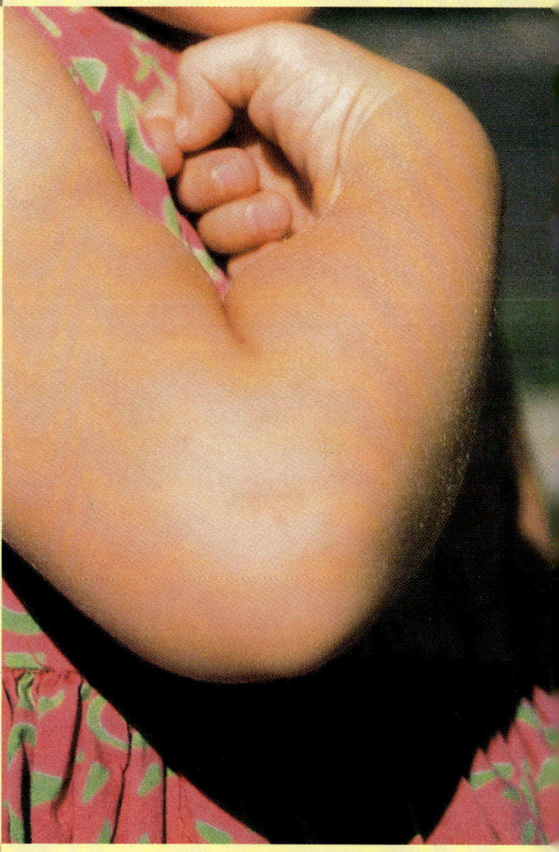

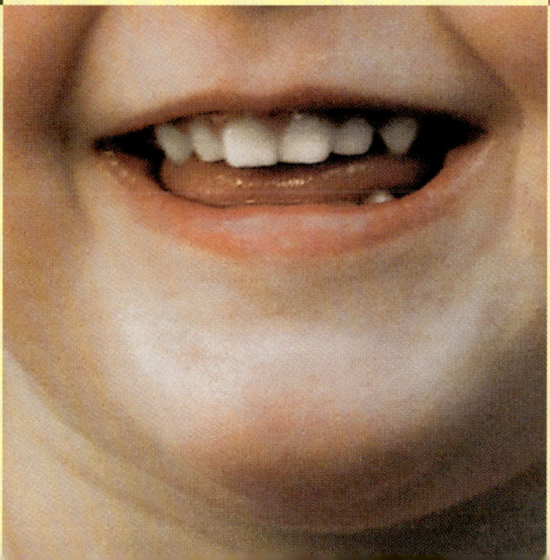

Finger, toe, elbow, knee

This is my BODY,
look at me!

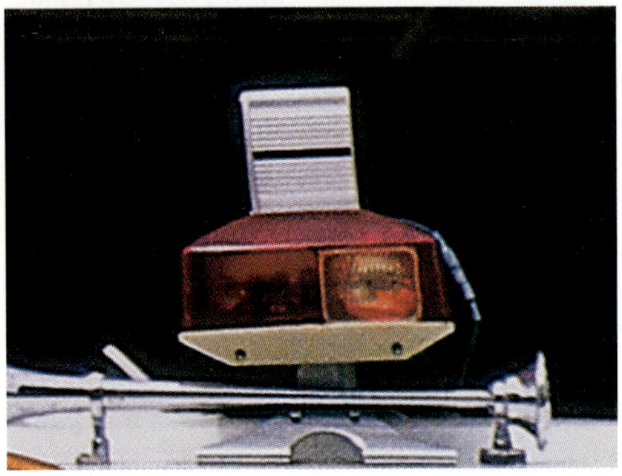

EMERGENCY
CALL 911

NORTHAMPTON Mack
ENGINE 4
EMERGENCY
CALL 911